the Margarita
party book

R&R PUBLICATIONS MARKETING PTY LTD

R&R Publications Marketing Pty. Ltd
12 Edward Street, Brunswick
Victoria 3056 Australia
Phone (61 3) 9381 2199 Fax (61 3) 9381 2689
Australia-wide toll free 1800 063 296
E-mail: info@randrpublications.com.au
Web: www.randrpublications.com.au
©Richard Carroll

Publisher: Richard Carroll
Designer: Aisling Gallagher
Photography and Styling: Brent Parker Jones
Food Stylist: Neil Hargreaves
Assistant Food and Drink Stylist: Lee Blaylock
Presentation: R&R PhotoStudio
Proofreader: Kate Evans

ISBN: 1 74022 596 1
EAN: 9 781740 225 960

First printed: May 2006
This edition printed January 2007
Printed in China by
Max Production Printing Ltd

Cover image: Frozen Blue Margarita, page 61

Contents

The History of the Margarita

The history of the margarita has been romanticized like very few other cocktails. There is a number of theories as to how the margarita emerged and how it got its name, several are rather convincing, but to this date no one story has proved inconclusively true.

A few of the stories of its creation:

- In the early 1930s, it was created at the Caliente Race Track in Tijuana.

- In 1936 Danny Negrete invented the drink for his girlfriend, Margarita, whilst working at the Garci Crespo Hotel.

- In 1938, Carlos Hererra invented the drink for Marjorie King, who apparently couldn't drink anything except tequila.

- On 4th July 1942, a customer requested barman Francisco Morales for a Magnolia, however he could not remember the recipe, so made up another drink and called it the 'Daisy' instead (which is Mexican for Margarita).

- In the 1940s, Enrique Bastante Gutierez created the drink for Rita Hayworth, who's real name was Margarita Carmen Cansino.

- In 1948 Margaret Sames created the drink for a special party.

- In 1948 it was created in Galveston, Texas, by Santos Cruz, who mixed it for Peggy Lee.

- In the early 1950s it was created at the Tail o' the Cock restaurant in Los Angeles in order to find a way to introduce Jose Cuervo tequila into the market.

The stories are endless, you can even make up your own!

The golden rule when assembling any cocktail, is to use a proper ratio of the ingredients used, in order to present a balance of flavors.

Mixing Margaritas

You may be confused when reading some cocktail books as many seem to want to put a special spin on making the perfect margarita. You have in this book the results of many years of margarita making and drinking, and we can assure you that if you follow the recipes within you will experience perfect margaritas every time.

A well-crafted margarita is tart and not too sweet, and served ice-cold in a salt-rimmed margarita glass. There are many variations including straight-up, on-the-rocks and frozen, all of them giving the recipient a wonderful taste sensation and all of them perfect to drink on a hot afternoon or evening.

In this book we use a radio of 3–2–1, which is 3 parts tequila, 2 parts triple sec and 1 part freshly squeezed lime juice. Always make sure that you have clean ice cubes and plenty of them!

The Ingredients

In the case of mixed cocktails it is acceptable to go for middle of the road ingredients; you do not have to go to the expense of buying the absolute top quality ingredient to get a very acceptable result. We always use Jose Cuervo blanco/silver tequila, and Cointreau as our ideal triple sec, and always choose freshly squeezed limes. You can use bottled juice but it's better to go for the freshly squeezed variery. Look for limes that have a little give in them when you squeeze; these tend to be juicer. Darker limes have a stronger flavor then the lighter ones. In the following pages l have explained each of the ingredients used in the recipes in more detail. This will allow you to go to your liquor store fully armed with the knowledge of which ingredients to buy to make your margarita party a real success.

The Equipment

Measure: A traditional jigger is a double-sided device. It has a large measure on one end, and a smaller one on the other. The larger measure is usually $1^1/_2$ oz/ 45mL, and is called a 'jigger'. The smaller side is usually 1 oz/30mL, and is referred to as a 'pony'.

Shaker: There are two popular types of cocktail shakers commonly used. The Cobbler Shaker is the classic cocktail shaker and is normally made of three pieces: a metal tumbler, a snug-fitting lid with a strainer, and a small cap that fits over the lid and covers the strainer. This is the type of shaker that most people will have at home because it is so simple and straightforward to use. The Boston Shaker is a variation on the Cobbler Shaker, and is what bartenders tend to use. This is a shaker whose lid doesn't have a built-in strainer, thus it only consists of two parts. One part is a metal mixing tumbler; the other is a slightly smaller glass tumbler (often just a pint-sized beer glass).

Strainer: As mentioned above some types of cocktails shakers already have a strainer integrated into their lids. While they do the job, it takes longer to pour out the drinks, and you end up spending time twirling the shaker around to get out all of the liquid. In our recipes we tend to use a Hawthorn Strainer. This is by far the most common type of cocktail strainer; it has a unique look to it, with a wire 'spring' that encircles the rim. The rolled spring keeps the ice in the shaker while still allowing some of the fruit pulp and even some small shards of ice into the glass. Traditionally you will find Hawthorn Strainers with either two or four prongs which stabilize it on the top of the shaker, but you can also find them without any prongs; these have just extra wide spring that will do the job.

Mixing glass: A large glass with a lip makes pouring easier. You can use the metal base of your shaker which is probably better as it chills the drink quicker than glass.

Bar spoon: A spoon with a long twisting handle which is ideal for stirring drinks in tall glasses or jugs.

Glasses: Cocktails can be poured into any glass but the better the glass the better the appearance of the cocktail. Try to avoid colored glasses as they spoil the appearance of the drinks. All cocktails glasses have been designed for a specific task:

Sugar Syrup

2 oz/60 mL water
1 cup sugar

Place sugar and water in a saucepan and bring to a boil. Reduce heat and simmer gently for approximately 5 minutes until the mixture condenses into a clear, sweet syrup. Cool. You can use immediately or store indefinitely in a sealed container in the refrigerator.

Sweet and Sour Mix

3 cups water
3 cups granulated sugar
2 cups fresh lemon juice
2 cups fresh lime juice

Combine water and sugar in a large saucepan. Stir over medium heat until sugar dissolves. Bring to the boil. Cool syrup. Mix syrup, lemon juice and lime juice in jug chill until cold. (Can be made 1 week ahead. Cover; keep chilled.) Makes 8 cups.

• Hi-ball glasses for long, cool, refreshing drinks.
• Cocktail glasses for short, sharp, or stronger drinks.
• Champagne saucers for creamy after-dinner style drinks.

The stem of the glass has been designed so you may hold it while polishing, leaving the bowl free of marks and germs. A proven method of cleaning glasses is to hold each glass individually over a bucket of boiling water until the glass becomes steamy and then with a clean linen cloth rub the glass in a circular motion.

The Techniques

Chilling the glass: All cocktail glasses should be kept in a refrigerator or filled with ice in order to chill the glass while you are preparing the cocktails. An appealing effect on a 3 oz/90mL cocktail glass can be achieved by running the glass under cold water and then placing it in the freezer.

Frosting the rim: This technique is used to coat the rim of the glass with either salt or sugar. First, rub a slice of lime, lemon or orange all the way around the glass rim. Then hold the glass by the stem upside down, rest it on a plate containing the salt or sugar and turn slightly so that it adheres to the glass. Pressing the glass too deeply into the salt or sugar often results in chunks sticking to the glass. A lemon or lime slice is used for salt and an orange slice is used for sugar. To achieve color effects, put a small amount of grenadine or colored liqueur in a plate and coat the rim of the glass, then gently place it in the sugar. The grenadine absorbs the sugar and turns it pink. This is much easier than mixing grenadine with sugar and then trying to get it to stick to the glass. When pouring liquid into the glass make sure you pour into the centre of the glass and do not spill any on the rim.

Shaking: To shake is to mix a cocktail by shaking it in a cocktail shaker. Place the ingredients into your shaker, add the cubed ice, seal and shake vigourously for 10–15 seconds. Then pour the contents straight into the glass.

Stirring and blending: To stir a cocktail is to mix the ingredients by stirring them with plenty of ice in a mixing glass or in the base of your shaker, and then straining them into a chilled cocktail glass. Short circular twirls are most preferred. Stir 30–40 times – this should be enough to chill the drink. Spirits, liqueurs and vermouths that blend easily together are mixed using this method.

For blended drinks simply mix the ingredients in a blender with crushed ice. If you are adding fruit, it is best to add it first. Slicing small pieces gives a smoother texture than if you add the fruit whole. The crushed ice should be added last; avoid using cubed ice as it may harm the motor in your blender. Blending the ingredients in this order ensures that the fruit is mixed freely with the alcoholic ingredients and the ice is mixed mix into the fruit and liquid gradually, chilling the cocktail.

Building the cocktail: To build a cocktail is to mix the ingredients in the glass in which the cocktail is to be served, floating one on top of the other.

Garnishing: Simplicity is the most important fact to keep in mind when garnishing cocktails.

Do not overdo the garnish; make it striking, but if you can't get near the cocktail to drink it then you have failed. Most world champion cocktails have just a lemon slice, or a single red cherry. A swizzle stick should be used in long cocktails. Straws are always served for a lady, but are optional for a man.

Liqueurs and Spirits

Amaretto almond liqueur is a rich subtle liqueur with a unique almond flavor.

Banana liquer is a sweet, intensely flavored banana liqueur.

Blackberry liqueur is a sweetened alcoholic beverage consisting of a base of alcohol and minimum 2.5% sugar, flavored and colored with blackberries. The liqueur is sweeter and lower in proof than blackberry-flavored brandy.

Blue Curacao liqueur is a sweet blue liqueur, distilled and flavored from the dried peel of bitter oranges. It can also contain distillates of lemons and curacao fruit, sugar and wine.

Calvados is a brandy made from distillate of apple cider or the pulps of special apples that grow in the Department of Calvados, in Normandy, France.

Chambord Liqueur is a sweet, red, raspberry-flavored French liqueur made from black raspberries, honey, fruits and herbs.

Champagne is sparkling wine that comes from the Champagne region of France. The word 'Champagne' is often incorectly used to refer to any form of sparkling wine.

Cherry Brandy is made from concentrated morello cherry juice.

Coconut liqueur is a smooth liqueur, composed of exotic coconut, heightened with light-bodied white rum.

Cointreau is a clear, brandy-based liqueur and type of triple sec flavored from the peel of sour and sweet oranges.

Creme de Cacao is a dark brown or clear chocolate-flavored liqueur made from the cacao seed.

Crème de Cassis is a deep, rich purple; it promises and delivers a regal and robust flavor and aroma.

Creme de Menthe is a sweet, white/green mint-flavored liqueur made from mint and spearmint.

Galliano is a sweet, yellow, Italian, herbal-flavored liqueur made with hints of anise, licorice and vanilla, as well as other herbs and spices.

Gin has an aroma comes from using the highest quality juniper berries and other rare and subtle herbs.

Grand Marnier is an orange flavored liqueur produced from a blend of cognac, orange peel, spices and vanilla.

Kahlua is a smooth, dark liqueur made from real coffee and fine clear spirits. Its origins are in Mexico.

Mango liqueur is flavored and colored with ripe mangoes and mixed with an alcohol base. A vibrant sunset color with an enigmatic mango taste. It's a very versatile liqueur, and it mixes well with other liqueurs or spirits.

Maraschino liqueur is made from marasca cherries, processed and distilled much like brandy, and then combined with a pure cane syrup, aged and filtered, and turned into a sweet cherry-infused liquor.

Midori melon liqueur is vibrant green in color, with a light, refreshing taste of melon.

Peach liqueur has a flavor of fresh peaches and natural peach juice which make it a cocktail lover's dream.

Peach Schnapps is a crystal clear, light liqueur, bursting with the taste of ripe peaches. Drink it chilled or on the rocks or mix it with any soft drink or juice.

Rum is a distilled spirit, made from fermented molasses which is made from sugarcane. Rum traditionally comes in three basic styles: white (or light); gold (or amber); and dark.

Strawberry liqueur has a fluorescent red, unmistakable strawberry bouquet. Natural liqueur delivers a true-to-nature, fresh strawberry flavor.

Tequila is a clear white liquor distilled from the juice of the blue agave plants grown in Mexico. The juices are extracted from the heart of the plant (*agave azu tequilana weber*) and are distilled twice.

Tia Maria is a dark, medium-bodied coffee liqueur made from a fine blend of cane spirit, Jamaican coffee, vanilla and sugar.

Triple Sec (meaning 'Triple distilled') is a strong, sweet and colorless orange flavored liqueur. It is made from the dried peel of oranges found on Curacao, an island in the Caribbean. Curacao, Grand Marnier and Cointreau are popular triple secs.

Vodka is a clear liquor manufactured from ethyl alcohol. It lacks color, and normally has very little taste or aroma. It is said to have been originally created from potatoes in Russia for medicinal purposes. Nowadays, vodka is distilled from barley, wheat or rye.

Mixers

Angostura bitters is made from a secret blend of rare tropical herbs and spices.

Grenadine is a strong red syrup made from redcurrants and pomegranates. It is a useful ingredient for many cocktails – acting as both a coloring and sweetener.

Lime/lemon juice is normally best freshly squeezed, and is an essential ingredient for cocktails. To get the most juice out of a fresh lime, bring it to room temperature and roll it under your palm against a hard surface before squeezing.

Orange bitters A bitter liquor made from the dried peel of unripe sour or bitter oranges, and steeped in gin or alcohol.

Sweet-and-sour mix is a blend of lemon juice and syrup. It is often just refered to as sour mix, and is available at most liquor stores but can easily be made (see the recipe on page 8).

Sugar syrup A lowly-heated mixture of sugar and water. See recipe on page 8.

Garnishes

Maraschino cherry A sugar syrup – coated cherry, dyed red and flavored with almond.

Margaritas

Traditional Margarita

The traditional margarita is based on a 3-2-1 principle: 3 parts tequila, 2 parts Cointreau, 1 part freshly squeezed lime juice, shaken with ice and strained into a margarita glass.

lemon slice
salt
$1\frac{1}{2}$ oz/45mL tequila
1 oz/30mL Cointreau
$\frac{1}{2}$ oz/15mL lime juice, freshly squeezed
ice
lemon slice, extra, to garnish

Rub margarita glass rim with lemon slice and frost with salt. Combine liquid ngredients with ice; shake well. Strain drink into glass. Garnish with slice of lemon and serve.

American Legion Margarita
(not photographed)

lime slice
salt
2 oz/60mL tequila
1 oz/30mL Cointreau
$\frac{1}{2}$ oz/15mL lemon juice, freshly squeezed
$\frac{1}{2}$ oz/15mL lime juice, freshly squeezed
ice
lime slice, extra, to garnish

Rub margarita glass rim with lime slice and frost with salt. Combine liquid ingredients with ice; shake well. Strain drink into glass. Garnish with slice of lime and serve.

Traditional Margarita

Apple Margarita

Apple Margaritas

lemon slice
salt
1 oz/30mL Calvados
1 oz/30mL Grand Marnier Rouge
1 oz/30mL grenadine

1 oz/30mL lemon juice
1 oz/30mL tequila
ice
lemon slices, extra, to garnish

Rub margarita glass rims with lemon slice and frost with salt. Combine liquid ingredients with ice; shake well. Strain drink into prepared glasses. Garnish each glass with a lemon slice and serve. Makes 3 cocktails.

Banana Margarita

lemon or lime slice
salt
1½ oz/45mL tequila
1 oz/30mL lime or lemon juice

1 oz/30mL banana liqueur
½ oz/15mL Cointreau
ice
banana slice, to garnish

Rub margarita glass rim with lime or lemon slice and frost with salt. Combine liquid ingredients with ice; shake well. Strain drink into glass. Garnish with banana slice and serve.

Blackberry Margarita

lemon or lime slice
salt
1½ oz/45mL tequila
1 oz/30mL blackberry liqueur

1½ oz/45mL lime juice
½ oz/15mL Cointreau
lime wedge
ice

Rub margarita glass rim with lime or lemon slice and frost with salt. Combine liquid ingredients with ice; shake well. Strain drink into glass. Garnish with lime wedge and serve.

Banana Margarita

Blackberry Margarita

Blackcurrant Margarita

lemon or lime slice
salt
1½ oz/45mL tequila
1 oz/30mL crème de cassis liqueur

1½ oz/45mL lime juice
½ oz/15mL Cointreau
ice
lime wedge

Rub margarita glass rim with lime or lemon slice and frost with salt.
Combine liquid ingredients with ice; shake well. Strain drink into glass.
Garnish with lime wedge and serve.

Blue Margaritas

lime slice
1 tsp coarse salt
4 oz/125mL tequila
1 oz/30mL triple sec
2 oz/60mL lime juice

2 oz/60mL blue curacao
1 tsp superfine (caster) sugar
ice cubes
2¼ in/5.5cm slices star fruit
1 lime, cut into wedges

Prepare glasses by rubbing margarita glass rims with lime slice and
frost with salt. Fill a cocktail shaker halfway with ice. Place tequilla,
triple sec, lime juice, blue curacao, and sugar in the shaker; shake hard
for 30 seconds. Fill the prepared glasses with ice cubes. Garnish each
with a slice of star fruit or a lime wedge. Makes 2 servings.

Cadillac Margarita

lime slice
salt
1½ oz/45mL tequila

1 oz/30mL Grand Marnier
⅓ oz/10mL lime juice
lime wedge, to garnish

Prepare glasses by rubbing margarita glass rims with lime slice and
frost with salt. Shake tequila with Grand Marnier and lime juice, and
strain into a prepared cocktail glass. Garnish with lime wedge.

Blackcurrant Margarita

Blue Margarita

Cadillac Margarita

Catalina Margarita

lime slice
salt
1½ oz/45mL gold tequila
1 oz/30mL peach schnapps
1 oz/30mL blue curacao
4 oz/125mL sweet and sour mix (see page 8)
ice
lime wedge, to garnish

Prepare glasses by rubbing margarita glass rim with lime slice and frost with salt. Mix all liquid ingredients with cracked ice in a shaker or blender and strain into the chilled prepared margarita glass. Garnish with lime wedge.

Chambord Margarita

lime or lemon slice
salt
1½ oz/45mL tequila
1 oz/30mL lime or lemon juice
1 oz/30mL Chambord liqueur
½ oz/15mL Cointreau
ice
lime quarter, to garnish

Rub margarita glass rim with lime or lemon slice and frost with salt. Combine liquid ingredients with ice; shake well. Strain drink into glass. Garnish with lime quarter and serve.

Catalina Margarita

Chambord Margarita

Cherry Margarita

Cherry Margarita

lime or lemon slice
salt
1½ oz/45mL tequila
1 oz/30mL maraschino liqueur
1½ oz/45mL lime juice, freshly squeezed
½ oz/15mL Cointreau
ice
lime wedge, to garnish

Rub margarita glass rim with lime or lemon slice and frost with salt. Combine liquid ingredients with ice; shake well. Strain drink into glass. Garnish with lime wedge and serve.

Citrus Margarita

lime or lemon slice
salt
2 oz/60mL tequila
1 oz/30mL lime juice, freshly squeezed
1 oz/30mL orange juice, freshly squeezed
1 oz/30mL Cointreau
ice
orange slice, to garnish

Rub margarita glass rim with lime or lemon slice and frost with salt. Combine liquid ingredients with ice; shake well. Strain drink into glass. Garnish with orange slice and serve.

Citrus Margarita

Cowboy Margarita

Cowboy Margaritas

$1\frac{1}{2}$ cups frozen limeade concentrate
$1\frac{1}{2}$ cups tequila
$1\frac{1}{2}$ cups beer
ice

Place undiluted frozen limeade concentrate in a jug. Fill empty limeade can with tequila and pour into the jug. Fill empty limeade can with beer and pour into the jug. Serve over plenty of ice. Makes about 4 big servings.

Cranberry Margarita

lemon slice
granulated sugar
$1\frac{1}{2}$ oz/45mL tequila
$3/4$ oz/25mL lemon juice

$3/4$ oz/25mL triple sec
$2\frac{1}{2}$ oz/75mL cranberry juice
5 ice cubes
lemon slices, extra, to garnish

Rub margarita glass rim with lemon slice and frost with sugar. Combine liquid ingredients with ice; shake well. Pour drink into glass. Garnish with lemon slice and serve.

Gold Margarita

lime or lemon slice
salt
2 oz/60mL gold tequila
$1\frac{1}{2}$ oz/45mL lime juice

$1/2$ oz/15mL Cointreau
ice
lime wedge, to garnish

Rub margarita glass rim with lime or lemon slice and frost with salt. Combine liquid ingredients with ice; shake well. Strain drink into glass. Garnish with lime wedge and serve.

Cranberry Margarita

Gold Margarita

Guava Margarita

lemon slice
granulated sugar
1½ oz/45mL tequila
¾ oz/25mL lemon juice

¾ oz/25mL triple sec
2½ oz/75mL guava juice
5 ice cubes

Rub margarita glass rim with lemon slice and frost with sugar. Combine liquid ingredients with ice; shake well. Pour drink into glass. Garnish with lemon slice and serve.

Jumping Margarita

slice of lime
salt
1½ oz/45mL tequila
1 oz/30mL triple sec
1½ oz/45mL margarita mix

½ oz/15mL lime juice
3 oz/90mL lemonade
ice
slice of lime, extra, to garnish

Rub margarita glass rim with lime slice and frost with salt. Mix the first 5 ingredients in shaker filled with ice; shake well. Strain cocktail into glass. Garnish with lime slice and serve.

Mango Margarita

lime or lemon slice
salt
1½ oz/45mL tequila
1 oz/30mL mango liqueur

1 oz/30mL lemon or lime juice
½ oz/15mL Cointreau
ice
lime or lemon slice, extra, to garnish

Rub margarita glass rim with lime or lemon slice and frost with salt. Combine liquid ingredients with ice; shake well. Strain drink into glass. Garnish with lime or lemon slice and serve.

Guava Margarita

Jumping Margarita

Mango Margarita

Midori Margarita

Midori Margarita

lime or lemon slice
salt
2 oz/60mL tequila
1 oz/30mL lime or lemon juice

1 oz/30mL Midori
ice
lemon or lime slice, extra, to garnish

Rub margarita glass rim with lime or lemon slice and frost with salt. Combine liquid ingredients with ice; shake well. Strain drink into glass. Garnish with slice of lime or lemon and serve.

Passionfruit Margaritas

lime slices
salt
3 cups passionfruit juice
1 lime, freshly squeezed

12 oz/340mL tequila
4 oz/125mL Grand Marnier
ice
raspberries, for garnish

Prepare glasses by rubbing margarita glass rims with lime slice and frost with salt. Combine liquid ingredients with ice; shake well. Store in the refrigerator until ready to use. Pour cocktail into glass over ice. Garnish with a few raspberries. Makes 6 margarita cocktails.

Peach Margarita

lime or lemon slice
salt
1½ oz/45mL tequila
1 oz/30mL lime or lemon juice

1 oz/30mL peach liqueur
½ oz/15mL Cointreau
ice
lemon or lime slice, extra, to garnish

Rub margarita glass rim with lime or lemon slice and frost with salt. Combine liquid ingredients with ice; shake well. Strain drink into glass. Garnish with slice of lime or lemon and serve.

Passionfruit Margarita

Peach Margarita

Pineapple Margarita

lime or lemon slice
salt
2 oz/60mL tequila
2 oz/60mL pineapple juice
1 oz/30mL lime or lemon juice, freshly squeezed
1 oz/30mL Cointreau
ice
pineapple spear, to garnish

Rub margarita glass rim with lime or lemon slice and frost with salt.
Combine liquid ingredients with ice; shake well. Strain drink into glass.
Garnish with pineapple spear and serve.

Strawberry Margarita (not photographed)

lime or lemon slice
salt
$1\frac{1}{2}$ oz/45mL tequila
1 oz/30mL lime or lemon juice, freshly squeezed
1 oz/30mL strawberry liqueur
$\frac{1}{2}$ oz/15mL Cointreau
ice
1 strawberry, to garnish

Rub margarita glass rim with lime or lemon slice and frost with salt.
Combine liquid ingredients with ice; shake well. Strain drink into glass.
Garnish with strawberry and serve.

Pineapple Margarita

Toledo Margarita (not photographed)

lime or lemon slice
salt
1 oz/30mL tequila
1 oz/30mL triple sec
$\frac{1}{2}$ oz/15mL fresh lemon juice
$\frac{1}{2}$ oz/15mL "Rose's" sweetened lime juice
ice
slice of lime or lemon, extra, to garnish

Rub margarita glass rim with lime or lemon slice and frost with salt.
Combine ingredients with ice; shake well. Strain drink into glass.
Garnish with lime or lemon slice and serve.

Vanilla Margarita (not photographed)

1 oz/30mL tequila
1 oz/30mL Grand Marnier
1 oz/30mL triple sec
1 (8–10 in/20–25cm) vanilla bean
ice
salt or sugar

Using an empty tequila bottle, put equal parts of the mixture into the
bottle. Add the vanilla bean, which you can purchase at health-food
stops. Let sit for at least 2 months; the longer it sits the better. Once
you open it, shake with ice, pour into glass and drink it on the rocks
(or blended if you prefer). You can frost rim of glass with either salt or
sugar, whichever you prefer.

Frozen Margaritas

How to Mix a Frozen Margarita

Break out the chips and salsa, you're making frozen margaritas! Call 'em 'blended' if you prefer, just serve them as soon as they're made for the best results.

lime slice

coarse salt

2 oz/60mL tequila

¾ oz/25mL lime juice

1 oz/30mL triple sec or Cointreau

1 cup crushed ice

lime wedge, to garnish

Prepare glasses by rubbing margarita glass rim with lime slice and frost with salt. Mix tequila, lime juice, triple sec or Cointreau and crushed ice in a blender and blend at medium speed for 5–10 seconds. Pour into prepared glass immediately. Garnish with lime wedge.

Tips: Variations of the frozen margarita include fruit. Cut the ice down to half a cup and add half of cup frozen fruit. Try peach, raspberry, cherry or strawberry liqueurs instead of triple sec and use the same fruit in the drink. Blend for 20 seconds, instead of 10, and garnish with appropriate fresh fruit. Some people don't like the salt on the glass, so you might ask first or use sugar.

Frozen Cherry Margarita

lime or lemon slice

salt

6 maraschino cherries

1½ oz/45mL tequila

1 oz/30mL lime juice

1 oz/30mL maraschino liqueur

ice

lime slices, extra, to garnish

Rub margarita glass rims with lime or lemon slice and frost with salt. In a blender, combine maraschino cherries, tequila, sugar, lime juice and maraschino liqueur. Blend until smooth. Add ice cubes a few at a time until the mixture becomes thick and slushy. Pour into prepared glasses. Garnish with lime or lemon slice and serve. Makes 2–4 cocktails.

Frozen Cherry Margarita

Frozen Double Apricot Margaritas

Frozen Double Apricot Margaritas

1¼ cups halved, pitted unpeeled apricots or 1 lb/500g canned unpeeled
  apricot halves (drained)
¼ cup tequila
2 oz/60mL granulated sugar
2 oz/60mL lime juice
2 oz/60mL apricot nectar
3 cups ice cubes
extra lime juice
coarse salt

lime or lemon slices, extra, to garnish

Rub margarita glass rims with lime or lemon slice and frost with salt. In
a blender, combine apricot halves, tequila, sugar, lime juice and apricot
nectar. Blend until smooth. Add ice cubes a few at a time until the
mixture becomes thick and slushy. Pour into prepared glasses. Garnish
with lime or lemon slice and serve. Makes 2–4 margarita cocktails.

Honeydew Margaritas

lime slice
salt
3 cups diced ripe honeydew melon
$\frac{1}{4}$ cup gold tequila
2 oz/60mL triple sec
2 oz/60mL lime juice
14 large ice cubes
6 lime wedges, to garnish

Rub margarita glass rims with lime slice and frost with salt. Blend melon, tequila, triple sec, lime juice and ice cubes until slushy. Pour into prepared glasses, then garnish each with a lime wedge. Makes 2–4 margarita cocktails.

Italian Margarita

lime or lemon slices
salt
$\frac{3}{4}$ cup frozen lemonade concentrate
3 oz/90mL tequila
2 oz/60mL amaretto
1 oz/30mL triple sec
3 oz/90mL water
3 cups ice cubes

Rub margarita glass rim with lime or lemon slice and frost with salt. Put all liquid ingredients and ice in a blender and blend until slushy. Pour drink into prepared glass. Garnish with lime or lemon slice and serve.

Honeydew Margarita

Italian Margarita

Frozen Strawberry Margarita

Frozen Strawberry Margaritas

lime or lemon slices
salt
¾ cup tequila
2 oz/60mL triple sec

¼ cup frozen limeade concentrate
1 cup frozen strawberries
8 cups crushed ice
lime or lemon slices, extra, to garnish

Rub margarita glass rim with lime or lemon slice and frost with salt. Combine ingredients in a blender and process until slushy. Pour drink into prepared glasses. Garnish with lime or lemon slice and serve. Makes 4 servings.

Kid-Friendly Margarita Punch

Don't leave the kids out of the fiesta! Make this fun and festive punch for them and other teetotallers. It is a great all-purpose punch that works perfectly with Mexican menus, grilled food, and any outdoor gathering. Instead of using egg whites, we now use meringue powder to make sure the punch is safe from any possible contamination with salmonella.

lemon or lime slice
salt
1½ cup frozen limeade concentrate
1½ cup frozen lemonade concentrate
1 cup superfine/caster sugar

equivalent of 4 egg whites
6 cups crushed ice
8 cups lemon lime soda
1 lime, thinly sliced
1 lemon, thinly sliced

Prepare glasses by rubbing margarita glass rims with lime or lemon slice and frosting with salt. Combine the concentrates, sugar, egg whites, and crushed ice in a large freezer-proof container. Cover tightly and freeze for at least one hour and up to a month. Place the frozen mixture into a large punch bowl. Slowly pour in the soda and add the lime and lemon slices. Makes 20 servings.

Kid Friendly Margarita Punch

Kiwi Margarita

Kiwi Margarita

lime slice
salt
½ cup silver tequila
½ cup triple sec
1 cup lemon juice, freshly squeezed
½ cup lime juice, freshly squeezed
½ cup superfine (caster sugar)
2 kiwifruit, peeled
crushed ice
lime wedges, to garnish

Rub margarita glass rims with lime slices and frost with salt. Put liquid ingredients, sugar and kiwifruit into a blender. On top of this mixture, pour crushed ice until blender is full. Blend until slushy. Pour into margarita glasses and garnish each with a lime wedge. Makes 2–4 margarita cocktails.

Lavender Margaritas

1 cup tequila
$\frac{1}{2}$ cup blue curacao
1 cup canned coconut milk
3 oz/90mL lime juice
1 lb/500g frozen unsweetened raspberries
1 lb/500g frozen unsweetened blueberries
4 cups ice cubes
1 tbsp granulated sugar
1 tsp fresh lavender blossoms
lime wedge
lavender sprigs, rinsed (optional)

In a blender, combine tequila, curacao, coconut milk, and lime juice. Cover and turn to high speed, then gradually add raspberries, blueberries, and ice. Whirl until margarita mixture is smooth and slushy. Depending on the size of your blender bowl you may have to blend in batches. Put sugar and lavender blossoms in a saucer. Rub with your fingers or mash with a spoon to release some of the lavender flavor. Rub glass rims with lime wedge to moisten. Dip rims in lavender sugar, coating evenly. Pour margaritas into sugar-rimmed glasses. Garnish with lavender sprigs. Will make 8–10 cocktails.

Lavender Margarita

Frozen Mango Margarita

Frozen Mango Margarita

lime wedge
sugar
1½ oz/45mL silver tequila
1 oz/30mL triple sec
1½ oz/45mL lemon juice, freshly squeezed
2 oz/60mL simple syrup or sweet-and-sour mix (see page 8)
¾ cup partially frozen mango, unsweetened (preferably individual
  quick frozen or fresh)
ice
mango slice, to garnish

Prepare glasses by rubbing margarita glass rim with lime wedge and
frost with sugar. Mix all liquid ingredients with mango and cracked ice
in a blender and blend until slushy. Pour cocktail into a chilled prepared
margarita glass. Garnish with mango slice.

Frozen Blue Margarita

(photograph on front cover)

lime wedge
1 tsp coarse salt
4 oz/125mL tequila
1 oz/30mL Cointreau
2 oz/60mL lime juice

2 oz/60 mL blue curacao
1 tsp superfine(caster sugar)
ice
2 starfruit slices to garnish

Prepare by rubbing the edge of two margarita glasses with the lime
wedge and frost with salt. Mix all ingredients (except starfruit and lime
wedge), in a blender filled with ice and blend until slushy. Pour cocktail
into the prepared margarita glass. Garnish with starfruit slice.

Frozen Papaya Margarita

lime slice
salt
2 papayas, peeled and chopped
1 cup gold tequila
$^3/_4$ cup triple sec
$^1/_2$ cup lime juice, freshly squeezed
crushed ice
4 slices of star fruit, for garnish

Prepare glasses by rubbing margarita glass rims with lime slice and
frost with salt. In a food processor, purée the papaya until smooth.
Using a rubber spatula, remove and place in a small container.
Refrigerate for 1 hour. In a blender, add half of the purée, half of
the tequila and triple sec and half the lime juice and fill with crushed
ice. Blend the mixture on high until thick and slushy. Pour into a jug.
Repeat with the remaining ingredients. Pour into the prepared glasses
and garnish with a piece of star fruit on the rim.
Makes 12 margarita cocktails.

Frozen Papaya Margarita

Frozen Watermelon Margaritas

2 lb/1 kg seedless watermelon,
  cut into 1 in/2½cm chunks
lime slice
salt
¾ cup tequila

½ cup triple sec
2½ oz/75mL fresh lime juice
ice
4 lime wedges, to garnish

Place the melon chunks in a plastic bag, and freeze until solid. Rub 4 margarita glass rims with lime slice and frost with salt. Transfer about three-quarters of the melon chunks, separating them, to a blender jar. Add the tequila, triple sec and lime juice then blend until fairly smooth. Add the remaining melon and ice and blend until smooth. Divide the cocktail mixture among the prepared glasses. Squeeze a lime wedge into each cocktail, drop the wedge into the glass, and serve immediately. Makes 4 cocktails.

Frozen Yucatan Margaritas with Tropical Fruit

12 lime wedges
2 tbsp granulated sugar
3 cups sweet-and-sour mix
  (see page 8)
1 cup tequila

¾ cup papaya nectar
¾ cup guava nectar
½ cup canned cream of coconut
16 ice cubes
12 lime slices, to garnish

Rub 12 margarita glass rims with lime wedge and frost with sugar. Combine half of the remaining ingredients (except lime slices) in a blender. Process until well blended. Pour into 6 glasses. Repeat with remaining half of the ingredients. Pour cocktail into remaining 6 glasses. Garnish each glass with lime slice on the side. Makes 12 margarita cocktails.

Frozen Watermelon Margarita

Frozen Yucatan Margarita with Tropical Fruit

Tequila Drinks

Acapulco

1 oz/30mL tequila
1 oz/30mL dark rum
1 oz/30mL tia maria

5 oz/150mL coconut cream
ice cubes
orange slice, to garnish

Shake liquid ingredients with ice and strain into a 10oz/285mL hi-ball glass. Serve garnished with an orange slice on side of glass.

Bloody Maria

ice cubes
$2\frac{1}{2}$ oz/75mL tequila
5 oz/150mL tomato juice
$\frac{1}{2}$ oz/15mL lemon juice

$\frac{1}{8}$ tsp black pepper
$\frac{1}{8}$ tsp celery salt
1 dash Tabasco sauce
1 stick of celery, to garnish

In a shaker half-filled with ice, combine all of the ingredients except the garnish. Shake well, then strain into a highball glass almost filled with ice cubes. Garnish with a stick of celery and a straw.

Earthquake

$1\frac{1}{2}$ oz/45mL tequila
1 tsp grenadine
2 strawberries
2 dashes orange bitters

crushed ice
lime slice, to garnish
strawberry, to garnish

Combine all ingredients, except garnish, in a blender for 15 seconds. Strain cocktail into a champagne glass and garnish with lime slice and a strawberry.

Acapulco

Bloody Mary

Earthquake

Exorcist

1½ oz/45mL tequila
¾ oz/25mL lime juice, freshly squeezed
¾ oz/25mL blue curacao
½ lime slice, to garnish

Combine all ingredients except garnish in a shaker, shake and strain into a 5 oz/150mL cocktail glass. Garnish with half a lime slice.

Gates of Hell

1½ oz/45mL tequila
2 tsp lemon juice, freshly squeezed
2 tsp lime juice, freshly squeezed
crushed ice
1 tsp cherry brandy, for drizzling

Combine all ingredients, except cherry brandy, in a shaker. Shake well. Strain into an old-fashioned glass almost filled with crushed ice. Drizzle the cherry brandy over the top.

Gorilla Sweat

½ tsp sugar
1½ oz/45mL tequila
boiling water
a dob of butter
ground nutmeg

Combine sugar and tequila into an old fashioned glass. Add boiling water and dob of butter and top with a shake of nutmeg.

Exorcist

Gates of Hell

Gorilla Sweat

Icebreaker

2 oz/60mL tequila
2 oz/60mL grapefruit juice
1 tsp grenadine
$\frac{1}{2}$ oz/15mL Cointreau
crushed ice

Combine all ingredients in a blender and blend for a few seconds.
Strain into a margarita glass.

Latin Lover

$1\frac{1}{2}$ oz/45mL champagne
  (or sparkling wine)
1 oz/30mL tequila

2 tsp lemon juice freshly squeezed
3 dashes grenadine
crushed ice

Combine all ingredients in a shaker and shake well. Strain into an ice-
filled old-fashioned glass.

Mexican Flag

2 oz/60mL tequila
2 tsp sugar syrup (see page 8)
2 tsp lime juice freshly squeezed
crushed ice
green, white and red cocktail onions, to garnish

Combine all ingredients except garnish in a shaker and shake well.
Pour into a champagne saucer. Garnish with green, white and red
cocktail onions on a toothpick across the glass.

Icebreaker

Latin Lover

Mexican Flag

Mexican Runner

1 oz/30mL tequila
½ oz/15mL tia maria
½ oz/15mL Grand Marnier
½ oz/15mL blackberry liqueur
half a banana

1 oz/30mL lime juice
crushed ice
2 strawberries, 1 to garnish
cocktail umbrella, to decorate

Blend all ingredients except garnish together and pour into a 10 oz/285mL cocktail glass. Garnish with strawberry and umbrella.

Midori Matadors

3 oz/90mL Midori
2 oz/60mL silver tequila
1 oz/30mL triple sec
3 oz/90mL lemon juice

2 tsp superfine (caster sugar)
crushed ice
2 lemon wedges, to garnish

Combine all ingredients, except garnish, in a cocktail shaker and shake well. Fill two 8 oz/250mL cocktail glasses with ice cubes. Strain the cocktail into the glasses evenly. Squeeze a lemon wedge into each glass and then drop the wedge into the glass to serve.

Mount Temple

1 oz/30mL Kahlua
1 oz/30mL tequila
1 oz/30mL coconut liqueur

ice
dollop of thick cream, to garnish

Build over ice in a 3 oz/90mL cocktail glass. Garnish with a dollop of cream in the centre of glass.

Mexican Runner

Midori Matador

Mount Temple

le

1 oz/30mL tequila
1 oz/30mL banana liqueur
2 tsp blue curacao
crushed ice
lemon wheel, to garnish

Stir over ice and strain into a 3 oz/90mL cocktail glass. Place a lemon wheel on side of glass to garnish.

Pinata

1 oz/30mL tequila
$\frac{1}{2}$ oz/15mL banana liqueur
1 oz/30mL lime juice, freshly squeezed
crushed ice

Combine all ingredients with ice and shake well. Pour into a 3 oz/90mL cocktail glass.

Rocket Fuel

ice
$\frac{1}{2}$ oz/15mL white rum
$\frac{1}{2}$ oz/15mL dry gin
$\frac{1}{2}$ oz/15mL vodka
$\frac{1}{2}$ oz/15mL tequila
1 oz/30mL 7-UP

Fill an 8 oz/250mL cocktail glass with ice and build using ingredients in order. Serve with a straw and swizzle stick.

Ole

Pinata

Rocket Fuel

Redheaded Stranger

1 tsp medium-hot salsa
1 tbsp pineapple purée
$^1/_2$ oz/15mL lime juice freshly squeezed
1 oz/30mL tequila
1 lime wedge

Drop the salsa into a 3 oz/90mL chilled cocktail glass. Next slowly pour in the pineapple purée. Gradually pour the lime juice over the back of a spoon into the cocktail, then repeat the process with the tequila. Suck on the lime wedge and sip the cocktail.

Scottie Was Beamed Up

crushed ice
1 oz/30mL tequila
$^1/_2$ oz/15mL Galiano
lemon twist, to garnish

Build over ice into an old-fashioned glass and garnish with a lemon twist.

Shady Lady

ice cubes
$1^1/_2$ oz/45mL tequila
$1^1/_2$ oz/45mL melon liqueur
5 oz/145mL grapefruit juice, freshly squeezed

Pour all of the ingredients into a highball glass almost filled with ice cubes and stir well.

Redheaded Stranger

Scottie Was Beamed Up

Shady Lady

Tequila Stinger

2 oz/60mL tequila
¹/₂ oz/15mL white crème de menthe
ice cubes

Combine the ingredients in a mixing glass half filled with ice cubes. Stir well and strain into a 5 oz/145mL cocktail glass.

Tequila Sunrise

1 oz/30mL tequila
1 tsp grenadine cordial
ice
orange juice
orange slice to garnish

Build tequila and grenadine over ice, then top up with orange juice. Garnish with orange slice, swizzle stick and straws.

Comments: Sipping this long cool cocktail at sunrise or sunset is magnificent. To obtain the cleanest visual effect, drop the grenadine down the inside of the glass after topping up with orange juice. Dropping grenadine in the middle creates a fallout effect, detracting from the presentation of the cocktail. Best served with chilled, freshly squeezed oranges.

Tequila Stinger

Tequila Sunrise

Tequila Sunrise no. 2

1 oz/30mL tequila
1 tsp lemon juice
$1/2$ oz/15mL Galliano Liqueur
cracked ice
$1/2$ oz/15mL banana liqueur
1 tsp grenadine cordial
1 orange slice, to garnish
2 maraschino cherries, to garnish

Shake all ingredients except garnishes in a cocktail shaker and strain into glass. Garnish with a slice of orange and cherries.

Toreador

2 oz/60mL tequila
1 oz/30mL dark crème de cacao
1 oz/30mL heavy cream
ice cubes
$1/4$ tsp unsweetened cocoa powder, to garnish

Combine the ingredients except garnish in a shaker half-filled with ice cubes. Shake well. Strain into a 5 oz/145mL cocktail glass and garnish with the cocoa powder.

Toreador

Party Tapas

Grilled Sea Scallop in Cos Spears **98**

Spanish Chicken Drumettes with Chorizo **101**

Duck with Olives and Sherry **102**

Beef Braised in Rioja **105**

Chicken Balls with Sweet Chili Sauce **106**

Spinach, Olive and Feta Frittata with Roasted Bell Pepper Sauce **109**

Shrimps with Spinach **110**

Lemon Chicken Fingers **113**

Baby Octopus Marinated in Olive Oil and Oregano **115**

Marinated Squid with Lemon and Herb Dressing **116**

Asparagus with Pecorino and Pancetta **119**

Potato Omelete **120**

Sesame Twists **122**

Grilled Sea Scallop in Cos Spears

1–1½ lb/450–650g sea scallops (approximately 12 scallops)
¼ cup couscous, cooked and fluffed
3 tbsp orange juice
2 tbsp olive oil
3 mixed baby cos leaves
2 blood oranges, peeled and segmented (squeeze and reserve juice)
2 oz/60g baby green beans, cleaned and cooked
1 large tomato, cored and diced
fresh cracked black pepper to taste

Coat scallops in cooked couscous. Season and grill scallops. Set aside and allow to cool. In a mixing bowl, combine orange juice and olive oil. Line up spears of baby lettuce leaves, top with sea scallops, blood orange segments, green beans and tomato. Season with fresh black cracked pepper and drizzle with dressing. Makes 12 pieces.

Grilled Sea Scallop in Cos Spears

Spanish Chicken Drumettes with Chorizo

Spanish Chicken Drumettes with Chorizo

8 chicken joints, such as thighs and drumsticks
2 tbsp olive oil
6 shallots, sliced
2 cloves garlic, crushed
1 red and 1 yellow bell pepper, deseeded and sliced
2 tsp paprika
$\frac{1}{4}$ cup dry sherry or dry vermouth
14 oz/400g canned chopped tomatoes
1 bay leaf
1 strip orange rind, pared with a vegetable peeler
$2\frac{1}{2}$ oz/75g chorizo, sliced
2 oz/60g pitted black olives
salt and black pepper to taste

Place chicken joints in a large, nonstick skillet and fry without oil for 5–8 minutes, turning occasionally, until golden. Remove chicken and set aside, then pour away any fat from the pan. Add oil to the pan and fry shallots, garlic and bell pepper for 3–4 minutes, until softened. Return chicken to the pan with the paprika, sherry or vermouth, tomatoes, bay leaf and orange rind. Bring to the boil then simmer, covered, over a low heat for 35–40 minutes, stirring occasionally, until chicken is cooked through. Add chorizo and olives and simmer for a further 5 minutes to heat through, then season with salt and pepper. Serve 2 joints with chorizo and pan ingredients onto 4 plates. Makes 8 small serves.

Duck with Olives and Sherry

½ cup large Spanish green olives, sliced or chopped
4 duck breasts, as much fat removed as possible
salt and freshly ground pepper
1 tbsp olive oil
1 medium onion, finely chopped
2 carrots, finely chopped
3 cloves garlic, minced
¾ cup chicken boullion
¼ cup dry sherry or white wine
¼ tsp fresh thyme
1 tbsp parsley, minced

Put olives in a small bowl, cover with warm water and set aside.
Preheat the oven to 350°F/180°C. Sprinkle duck with salt and pepper.
Place it in a roasting pan and prick it all over with a fork. Roast for 1
hour. Meanwhile, heat oil in a shallow flameproof casserole dish and
sauté onion, carrots and garlic over medium-high heat until onion
has wilted. Cut duck into serving pieces. Transfer the pieces to the
casserole. Pour off the fat in the roasting pan and deglaze the pan with
chicken boullion, scraping up any particles stuck to the bottom. Strain
the liquid into the casserole. Drain olives and add to the casserole
along with sherry, thyme, parsley and salt and pepper. Bring to the
boil on top of the stove, then cover and cook in the oven for 1 hour.
Makes 10 small servings.

Duck with Olives and Sherry

Beef Braised in Rioja

Beef Braised in Rioja

3 tbsp olive oil
24 oz/680g stewing beef, trimmed of fat and cut into 2 ½ in/6cm chunks
6 shallots, finely chopped
2 cloves garlic, crushed
2 sticks celery, thickly sliced
11 oz/310g mushrooms, thickly sliced
½ tsp ground allspice
½ bottle full-bodied red wine
1 cup tomato purée
2 sprigs fresh thyme
salt and black pepper

Preheat the oven to 350°F/180°C. Heat oil in a flameproof casserole
dish or large saucepan and fry meat over a high heat, stirring, for 5–10
minutes or until browned. Remove from the pan. Add shallots, garlic and
celery to pan and cook, stirring, for 3–4 minutes, until lightly browned.
Add mushrooms and cook for 1 minute or until softened. Stir in allspice,
wine, tomato purée and 1 sprig of thyme, and season with salt and pepper.
Return meat to the dish or pan and bring to a simmer. Cover and cook
in the oven or over a low heat on the stove for 1½ –2 hours, until beef
is tender. Season again if necessary, then serve garnished with remaining
thyme. Makes 8 small serves.

Chicken Balls with Sweet Chilli Sauce

1 lb/500g ground chicken meat
½ tsp salt
¼ cup dried breadcrumbs
1 medium onion, finely chopped
1 tbsp chopped cilantro
1 tbsp mild curry paste
1 egg
1 cup all-purpose flour
½ tsp salt and pepper combined
¼ cup canola oil
½ cup sweet chili sauce for dipping

Place chicken in a bowl and add salt, breadcrumbs, onion, cilantro, curry paste and egg. Mix together very well with a wooden spoon. Let rest for 10–20 minutes to allow absorption of juices before shaping. Take a heaped teaspoon of mixture and with wet hands roll into a ball and repeat until all balls are made. Place on a tray ready to fry. Mix flour and seasoning together; sprinkle onto on a flat plate or sheet of baking paper. Heat oil in a wide heavy-based frying pan. Roll each ball into the flour; shake off excess and place in pan. Do not crowd pan and adjust heat where necessary to fry at a steady pace. Turn balls frequently and roll whilst frying to keep a good round shape. Remove as they cook and drain on kitchen paper. Serve chicken balls on a platter and provide the sweet chili sauce in a bowl for dipping. Makes about 30 small balls.

Chicken Balls with Sweet Chilli Sauce

Spinach, Olive and Feta Frittata with Roasted Capsicum Sauce

Spinach, Olive and Feta Frittata with Roasted Bell Pepper Sauce

10 eggs
1 tbsp fresh oregano, chopped
black pepper, freshly cracked
$\frac{1}{4}$ cup olive oil
7 oz/200g potatoes, peeled and diced
1 brown onion, diced
1 clove garlic, crushed
5 oz/150g baby spinach
2 oz/60g pitted Kalamata olives, halved
2 oz/60g feta, crumbled
2 oz/60g semi-dried tomatoes
3 large red bell pepper

Lightly whisk together the eggs and oregano in a bowl, and season with black pepper. Set aside. Heat the oil in a $8\frac{3}{4}$ in/22cm pan and sauté the potatoes, onion and garlic for a few minutes (until soft). Add the spinach and cook until it begins to wilt. Remove the pan from the heat, then add olives, feta and semi-dried tomatoes. Return the pan to a very low heat, pour in the egg mixture, and cook for 10–15 minutes. Run a spatula around the sides of the pan as the frittata is cooking, and tilt it slightly so that egg mixture runs down the sides a little. When frittata is almost cooked through the middle, place under a grill for 5 minutes to cook and brown the top. Cut in wedges or squares with a drizzle of the roasted pepper sauce on top.

For the sauce: halve the pepper and remove the seeds. Chargrill the bell pepper (or broil) until black. Let them cool, and remove the skins. Place into a food processor and process until puréed. Transfer to a bowl. Makes $\frac{1}{2}$ cup. Serves 16–18 pieces.

Shrimps with Spinach

3½ oz/100mL olive oil
1 medium onion, diced
1 red bell pepper, deseeded and diced
1 clove garlic, crushed
2 tomatoes, peeled and diced
1½ bunches English spinach, washed and roughly chopped
2 tbsp dry white wine
juice of 1 lemon
salt and freshly ground black pepper
1 lb/500g shrimps, shelled and deveined
lemon wedges, to garnish

Heat two tablespoons of olive oil in a saucepan, and brown onion.
Add red bell pepper, garlic and tomatoes, and cook for 7 minutes. Add
spinach, white wine, lemon juice and seasoning. Cover and simmer
gently for 8–10 minutes (until spinach is tender). Remove from heat.
Stir and keep warm. Add the remaining oil to a large frying-pan.
Once hot, add shrimps and sauté, stirring constantly, for 3 minutes or
until just cooked. Spoon the shrimps into the spinach mixture, fold
to combine, and spoon onto a warm serving platter, garnished with
lemon wedges. Serve immediately. Serves 4.

Prawns with Spinach

Lemon Chicken Fingers

2 lb/1 kg chicken breast fillets
oil for deep frying

Marinade

2 tbsp soy sauce
¼ cup sherry
2 tsp grated fresh ginger
2 tsp lemon zest
2 tsp sugar

Batter

2 egg whites
¼ cup all purpose flour
¼ cup lemon juice

Dipping sauce

reserved marinade
½ cup chicken bouillon
2 tbsp lemon juice
2 tbsp cornstarch

Cut the breast fillets into ⅜-in/1cm wide strips from the long side of the fillet. Place strips in a non-metal dish. Combine marinade ingredients, pour over chicken strips, mix well and allow to marinate for 30 minutes. To make the batter, stiffly beat the egg whites to soft peaks, fold in flour and lemon juice. Remove the strips from marinade, reserving the marinade. Heat oil in a deep fryer to 350°F/180°C. Dip a few strips at a time into the batter and deep fry them for 5 minutes until golden. Drain on absorbent paper. Repeat with remainder. Pour reserved marinade into a saucepan, add chicken stock and bring to the boil. Mix to a smooth paste the lemon juice and cornflour, stir into the saucepan, lower heat and stir until sauce boils and thickens. Drizzle sauce over chicken fingers and serve. Serves 4.

Baby Octopus Marinated in Olive Oil and Oregano

Baby Octopus Marinated in Olive Oil and Oregano

⅓ cup olive oil
rind of 1 lemon
2 tbsp lemon juice
⅓ cup shallots, finely sliced
2 tsp oregano, chopped
freshly ground black pepper and salt
1½ lb/750g baby octopus, cleaned
salad leaves, for serving

In a bowl, mix together the olive oil, lemon rind, lemon juice, shallots, oregano, and pepper and salt. Add the octopus, and leave to marinate for 1 hour. Heat a chargrill pan, lightly brush with oil, add octopus, and cook, basting with marinade for 2–3 minutes, or until tender. Serve on a bed of salad leaves. Serves 4.

Marinated Squid with Lemon and Herb Dressing

3 oz/90mL lemon juice
3 cloves garlic, crushed
$\frac{1}{2}$ cup olive oil, extra for cooking
2 lb/1 kg squid, cut into thin rings

Dressing
2 oz/60mL lemon juice
$3\frac{1}{2}$ oz/100mL olive oil
$1\frac{1}{2}$ tbsp parsley, chopped
1 garlic clove, crushed
1 tsp Dijon mustard
salt and black pepper

Place lemon juice, garlic and oil in a bowl, add the squid, and marinate (for at least 3 hours). If time permits, marinate overnight. To make the dressing, place all ingredients in a bowl or jar and whisk well (until dressing thickens slightly). Heat 1 tablespoon of oil in a pan, add the squid, and cook for a few minutes, until calamari are cooked through. Alternatively, the squid can be cooked on chargrill plate. Serve squid with lemon and herb dressing drizzled over.
Serves 4–6.

Marinated Calamari with Lemon and Herb Dressing

Asparagus with Pecorino and Pancetta

Asparagus with Pecorino and Pancetta

1 lb/500g asparagus
8 thin slices of pancetta, cut into pieces
pecorino cheese, shaved

Dressing
juice of 1 lemon
3$\frac{1}{2}$ oz/100mL extra virgin olive oil
sea salt
black pepper, freshly ground

Trim off the thick ends of the asparagus and cook in boiling water for 4 minutes, until tender, but still crisp. Run under cold water, until asparagus is cool, then dry with paper towel. For the dressing, place the lemon in a bowl then slowly add the oil, whisking, until dressing is thick. Season with salt and pepper. Pour the dressing over asparagus, and serve with the pancetta and pecorino cheese shavings. Serves 4–6.

Potato Omelete

2 lb/1 kg potatoes, peeled
1 small onion, peeled (optional)
1 cup olive oil
5 eggs, beaten
salt

Wash and dry potatoes, then cut into thin slices. If you are using onion, dice it finely. Heat oil in a frying pan, add potatoes and onion, season and cover. Fry gently, moving the pan so that vegetables don't stick. Once potatoes are cooked (take care they don't become crisp) break them up a bit and remove from the pan with a slotted spoon. Add to the beaten eggs. Stir potatoes around until they are well covered with egg. Add salt to taste. Remove most of the oil from the frying pan, leaving about 1 tablespoon, and reheat. Have ready a plate with a slightly larger diameter than the pan. Return egg and potato mixture to the pan and cook for a few minutes until one side is golden. Next, and this is slightly tricky, slip the omelete out onto your plate, cooked-side down, and then slip it back into the pan, cooked-side up. Cook until firm. Your omelete should be about 2 in/5cm thick. If you are using it for tapas, then cut it into squares. Serves 6–8.

Potato Omelette

Sesame Twists

2 sheets of readymade puff pastry
2 oz/60g butter, melted
2 tbsp poppy seeds
2 tbsp sesame seeds
2 tbsp grated Parmesan cheese

Cut the pastry sheets in half. Brush with melted butter. Combine the poppy seeds, sesame seeds and cheese and sprinkle over pastry. Press the pastry firmly into pastry with a rolling pin. Using a sharp knife, cut widthwise into strips $\frac{3}{4}$ in/2cm wide and 4 in/10cm long. Twist strips slightly. Place onto a lightly greased baking tray and bake in a hot oven, 350°F/180°C, for 8 minutes.

Sesame Twists

Notes

Notes

Notes

Notes

Index